Kid ethics from a to z

By

James "Bud" Bottoms

An A to Z primer in character education. Designed to help young people learn the principles of considerate behavior and to instill in them a sense of responsibility and conscience.

ISBN: 978-0-9794863-0-2

For more information, visit www.SummerlandPublishing.com.

Printed in the U. S. A.

Introduction

Much like learning the alphabet, I feel that children should be exposed to the formal education of ethics at a very early age to help them socialize in appropriate and respectful ways. Childhood is a time when these future citizens should acquire the skills and attitudes that result in respect and proper decorum.

This is also a workbook designed to incorporate basic skills such as reading, writing, and spelling into the child's development of ethical principles.

The whimsical cartoons and rhymes not only define the word but encourage the reader to think about that word. This is followed with a question which asks the student to think and to express the meaning and application of each word.

The cartoons may be colored and enhanced by the child, serving as a reinforcing reminder of the ethics being described.

My sincerest hope is that "Kid Ethics" will help develop thoughtful, respectful, and caring citizens. We use ethics every day, all of our lives. That's why one of the best features of this book is that it encourages the whole family to participate in these essential values.

Thank you,

James "Bud" Bottoms

Dedication

This book is dedicated to those children, their parents, their schools, teachers and principals, and retirement homes and elders who participated in the survey of over 70 ethical words which eventually resulted in the making of "Kid Ethics."

For their editing advice and help, I want to thank:

The Rev. Carole Ann Cole
Matt Giamporcaro
Patty and Mike Moropoulos
Darcy and Bill Sylvester
Jolinda Pizzirani

Kid ethics
from a to z

By

James "Bud" Bottoms

An A to Z primer in character education. Designed to help young people learn the principles of considerate behavior and to instill in them a sense of responsibility and conscience.

appreciation

After dinner we make our wishes,
Clear the table, and do the dishes.

A
is for Appreciation

Early Thanksgiving morning, before the sun rises, our mom gets up and goes into the kitchen to prepare the turkey dinner for our big family. She bakes three big pies: apple, pumpkin, and pecan, to be served as a hot dessert. She stuffs the turkey with yummy herbs and puts it in the oven to roast. She cooks the cranberries into a sweet and chunky sauce. She turns dough into twenty-four golden rolls – hot and ready to butter. She steams a colorful rainbow of vegetables, and then mashes cooked potatoes into a big, white fluffy cloud. It takes all day and a lot of work to make Thanksgiving dinner for our big family and friends, but mom says she loves to do it because it's her way of showing **appreciation** for a wonderful family.

To show our **appreciation** for our mom, we clear the table and wash all the dishes while mom and the folks go into the living room to visit and rest their full tummies.

APPRECIATION • APPRECIATION • APPRECIATION • APPRECIATION • APPRECIATION • APPRECIATION • APPRECIATION

When someone is nice to you, how do you show your **appreciation**?

_____

_____

_____

balance

When you balance work with play,
You make the most of every day.

B

Is for Balance

The coach told Benny he was kicked off the basketball team. The school had a rule that said if your grades weren't good enough, you couldn't be on a team.

Benny loved sports more than anything; he played basketball, baseball, soccer, and football. When he wasn't playing team sports, he skateboarded, played tennis and went fishing.

In fact, he spent too much time playing and was always tired. He would eat dinner and then go right to bed, and not do his homework.

By not being on the basketball team, he wasn't so tired anymore which gave him more time to do his homework. Wanting to get back on the team, he studied hard.

In a few weeks, his grades improved, and he was allowed back on the court just in time for the championship game. Benny was so eager to play that he made the most baskets and helped to win the championship.

His desire to play sports taught him to **balance** his homework with play.

BALANCE • BALANCE • BALANCE • BALANCE • BALANCE • BALANCE • BALANCE • BALANCE • BALANCE • BALANCE

How do you **balance** your time for school and play?

_____

_____

_____

compassion

Caring and a kindly deed
Helps out those who are in need.

C

Is for Compassion

Mrs. Kong's cat "Tiger" got chased up a telephone pole by a big dog. Mrs. Kong called for him to come down, but he was too scared to move. She put a saucer of milk by the telephone pole, hoping he'd come down in the night. But he didn't budge. He just howled and meowed, keeping the neighbors awake all night.

The next morning, everybody wanted to help Mrs. Kong to get Tiger down. Someone called the fire department for help.

Soon a big fire truck arrived with a long ladder. A fireman climbed to the top of the telephone pole. It took a lot of time and patience to rescue Tiger, but at last he was down and safe in the arms of Mrs. Kong. The neighbors and the fireman had shown great care and **compassion** for Mrs. Kong and Tiger. Mrs. Kong showed her appreciation by baking a big cherry pie for everyone.

COMPASSION • COMPASSION • COMPASSION • COMPASSION • COMPASSION • COMPASSION • COMPASSION

When did you show **compassion** to help someone?

_____

_____

_____

determination

Because I tried with all my might,
I finally learned to ride my bike.

D

Is for Determination

Pedro got his first two-wheeled bicycle for Christmas. He tried to ride it, but he kept falling over. His dad bought him some training wheels to help him keep his balance. This gave him confidence that he could ride a two-wheeler.

Pedro's friends were already riding their bikes without training wheels, doing "wheelies," jumps, and riding on dirt trails. Pedro was **determined** to join them, so every morning he would get up early and practice balancing on his bike.

His patience and **determination** paid off. After only three weeks he could balance on two wheels. Pedro's dad took off the training wheels, and Pedro proudly rode off to join all his friends doing "wheelies."

DETERMINATION • DETERMINATION • DETERMINATION • DETERMINATION • DETERMINATION • DETERMINATION

Tell when you made up your mind and were **determined** to do something.

_____

_____

_____

empathy

When you are sad,
I'll help make you glad.

E

Is for Empathy

When Timmy arrived at the zoo, he immediately ran to see Ozzie, his favorite animal, who made him laugh by leaping wildly from swing to swing while howling loudly. But this day Ozzie sat in the corner, sad and all by himself with nobody to play with.

Ozzie the orangutan was very sad because Olga, his mate, was sick in the zoo hospital. Timmy had **empathy** for Ozzie. He understood that Ozzie was sad because he felt so lonely. So Timmy decided to visit with Ozzie all day until the zoo closed.

The next day, when Timmy returned to see Ozzie, the zoo-keeper told Timmy that Ozzie had perked up. He said that Ozzie was feeling better because Timmy had spent time with him and kept him company while Olga was getting well. Timmy was glad that he was able to make his friend feel better. After that, Timmy visited Ozzie every day to keep him company until Olga got well.

EMPATHY • EMPATHY • EMPATHY • EMPATHY • EMPATHY • EMPATHY • EMPATHY • EMPATHY • EMPATHY • EMPATHY

When a friend is happy or sad, how do you share his or her feelings and show **empathy**?

_____

_____

_____

forgiveness

Best to forgive for a wrong;
You might need some before too long.

F

Is for Forgiveness

Clara was eating her breakfast, when her dog, Bobo, snuggled up to her to say "good morning." His big, furry body accidentally bumped against the kitchen table and knocked her breakfast onto the floor. At first, Clara was so angry she yelled at Bobo, which made him feel sad. He groaned and curled up by her feet. This made Clara feel bad that she had scolded Bobo.

Then she remembered that she, too, had accidents, so she showed **forgiveness** and let him lick up the spilled cereal and milk. Bobo cleaned the floor and Clara felt much better about herself for **forgiving** Bobo.

After all, it was an accident and Bobo was her best friend.

FORGIVENESS • FORGIVENESS • FORGIVENESS • FORGIVENESS • FORGIVENESS • FORGIVENESS • FORGIVENESS

When did you show **forgiveness** to someone who had made you angry?

_____

_____

_____

generosity

All of us can show we care
By finding special gifts to share.

G
Is for Generosity

Flowers were in bloom, and fruit trees were blossoming. It was spring, and "Harold" the honeybee was very busy darting from flower to flower and from tree to tree. He was helping to pollinate the trees so that they would be fertile and bear fruit. At the same time, he was collecting honey to store for his family who lived in a hive in a big old tree.

"Brownie" the bear had just come out of hibernation, after sleeping all winter. He was very, very hungry. The first thing he wanted to eat was honey, so he headed for Harold's tree, knowing some would be stored there.

When Harold saw how hungry Brownie was, he **generously** shared his honey with him. The honey filled Brownie up, and gave him energy to go looking for berries in the forest.

Mother Nature reminds all of us to be helpful and **generous** because all things in nature are connected, and everything depends on everything else to live and to survive.

GENEROSITY • GENEROSITY • GENEROSITY • GENEROSITY • GENEROSITY • GENEROSITY • GENEROSITY

When did you help someone and show your **generosity**?

_____

_____

_____

honesty

Be honorable, truthful, and real,
And you'll like the way you look and feel.

H

Is for Honesty

Bodie's school was having its annual fair and was raffling off a new skateboard. Bodie hadn't bought a raffle ticket, but as he passed by a mud puddle, he found a raffle ticket sticking out of the mud. He picked it up just as the principal announced the winning numbers for the new skateboard. To his great surprise, the numbers matched the numbers on this ticket.

At first, he shouted with glee. Then being **honest**, Bodie told how he had found the winning ticket. The principal asked over the loud speaker if anybody had lost a ticket. Bridget, one of Bodie's classmates who had been playing in the mud puddle, raised her muddy little hand and won the skateboard.

Bridget and her parents thanked Bodie for his **honesty**, and the principal awarded Bodie with the Student of the Month Award. Everyone cheered for him, and he felt happy for Bridget and very proud of himself for being **honest**.

HONESTY • HONESTY • HONESTY • HONESTY • HONESTY • HONESTY • HONESTY • HONESTY • HONESTY • HONESTY

What does **honesty** mean to you?

_____

_____

_____

integrity

Keep your promise when you borrow;
Bring back what you took tomorrow.

I

Is for Integrity

Last night, a spooky noise scared Mrs. Cluck off her nest and she couldn't lay her daily egg. The next morning she asked her neighbor, Jenny Plenty, if she could borrow one of her eggs to help her relax, so that she could lay her own. She promised to return it the next day.

The next morning Mrs. Cluck had laid two eggs. She kept her promise and showed she had **integrity** by returning the borrowed egg. She also thanked Jenny Plenty for her help and compassion.

INTEGRITY • INTEGRITY • INTEGRITY • INTEGRITY • INTEGRITY • INTEGRITY • INTEGRITY • INTEGRITY • INTEGRITY

Tell how you kept a promise that showed you had **integrity**.

_____

_____

_____

justice

Judging fairly is the rule
For keeping everybody cool.

J

Is for Justice

The Clobbers were playing the White Shorts for the World Series. It was the end of the ninth inning, the bases were loaded, the score was tied, and the call was three balls and two strikes on the batter!

The players and the crowd were excited. Big Ben of the Clobbers was up to bat. He picked up his bat, looked down on home base, and kicked the dirt as he always did. Except this time, some dust flew into the catcher's face, which caused him to sneeze just as the pitch came across home plate. The catcher's sneeze startled Big Ben so that he accidentally swung at the ball.

Because of this, Big Ben lost his cool and started an argument with the catcher. However, the umpire jumped in between them and stopped their angry words. He said that it was an accident and neither player was to blame; that it wasn't a strike or a ball; and he told the pitcher to throw the ball again.

The umpire was fair, and **justice** was served. He asked the players to forgive each other and to "play ball!"

JUSTICE • JUSTICE • JUSTICE • JUSTICE • JUSTICE • JUSTICE • JUSTICE • JUSTICE • JUSTICE • JUSTICE • JUSTICE

Tell when were you treated fairly and felt that **justice** was served?

_____

_____

_____

kindness

Be nice to all animals, people, and plants,
Including snails, snakes, spiders, and ants.

K

Is for Kindness

Buddy loved to play in the garden. He liked to plant seeds and watch them grow. But most of all, he was fascinated by all the little creatures who lived in his garden.

He would put out food for the ants and watch their long line run back and forth carrying crumbs bigger than they were. Buddy's mom said she liked him to feed the ants outside because it kept them out of her house.

Buddy would spend hours watching a garden spider make the most beautiful webs. When it rained, the webs would catch droplets of water and glisten like diamonds. He would laugh when he watched a snail pull in its feelers and curl back into its shell-house.

Once, he found a colorful little garden snake which he put around his neck and shared it with his friends, and then put it back where he had found it.

Buddy showed his appreciation for all of nature's gifts by being thoughtful and **kind** to everything that flew, grew, crept, crawled, or slithered. They were his friends and playmates.

KINDNESS • KINDNESS • KINDNESS • KINDNESS • KINDNESS • KINDNESS • KINDNESS • KINDNESS • KINDNESS

What can you do today to show **kindness**?

_____

_____

_____

love

Happiness is being close
To people whom you love the most.

L

Is for Love

Elizabeth was puzzled about the word **"love"** because it seemed to have many meanings. So she counted them.

* Her mother said she **loved** music.

* Her dad **loved** playing golf.

* Grandma **loved** her church and helping the poor.

* Grandpa **loved** his country and reading the newspaper.

* Aunt Patty **loved** teaching children and eating chocolate.

* Uncle Matt **loved** his old hat and fishing.

She finally decided there were many kinds of **love**. She loved her dolls, her kitty and her bedroom, but best of all was the feeling of **love** she had for her mom and dad. And she showed her **love** by helping out around the house without being asked.

LOVE • LOVE • LOVE • LOVE • LOVE • LOVE • LOVE • LOVE • LOVE • LOVE • LOVE • LOVE • LOVE • LOVE • LOVE • LOVE

How do you show others that you **love** them?

_____

_____

_____

manners

Being thoughtful and polite
Is good behavior day and night.

M

Is for Manners

Saren prepared a beautiful tea party with her nicest tea set. She seated her guests, Tag the dog and Missy the kitty, in their proper places and politely poured them each a cup of milk. At first they showed good **manners**, and stayed seated, although they did make a lot of loud lapping and licking noises.

But when Tag finished his milk, he rudely nosed Missy kitty aside and began drinking her milk too. Missy got angry and leaped from her chair onto the table, pulling the tablecloth and the cups and saucers off the table. Tag and kitty showed bad **manners**, made a mess, and ruined the whole tea party.

It took a lot of patience, but being a good hostess and demonstrating good **manners**, Saren forgave her guests as she cleaned up the mess. After all, they were her best friends.
Learning good **manners** takes a lot of practice until they become good habits.

MANNERS • MANNERS • MANNERS • MANNERS • MANNERS • MANNERS • MANNERS • MANNERS • MANNERS

What are some ways you show good **manners**?

_____

_____

_____

nurture

With tender, loving care from mom,
A baby kangaroo grows strong.

N

Is for Nurture

When Joey, the kangaroo, was born, he was no bigger than a pink jelly bean. He lived, ate, and slept in his mom's soft, warm tummy-pouch. His mother's milk made him grow fast and strong, and soon he was ready to explore the world outside of his mom's pouch.

On his first adventure, he was learning how to balance himself on his big tail and how to hop on his long legs and big feet. His mother stayed close by and kept a watchful eye out for danger. Suddenly, she saw a pack of dingos, the wild dogs of Australia, hunting for food. The dingos saw Joey and thought he would make a tasty dinner.

When mother kangaroo saw the dingos coming toward her baby, she quickly scooped Joey up back into her pouch and bounded off into the forest outback, leaving the dogs far behind. Not only did mother kangaroo feed and comfort Joey, she also protected him from harm. Her **nurturing** helped him to grow into a big, strong kangaroo who could soon take care of himself.

NURTURE • NURTURE • NURTURE • NURTURE • NURTURE • NURTURE • NURTURE • NURTURE • NURTURE • NURTURE

How do you look after and **nurture** a person or pet?

_____

_____

_____

open-mindedness

A mind that's closed is just like broken;
Parachutes work best when they're open.

O

Is for Open-mindedness

From the very first time she'd ever seen a parachuter, Eudora the elephant wanted to do it too. She had this wonderful vision of floating down to earth from an airplane high in the sky. But every time she'd ask, people would laugh and discourage her. They would say that she was too big, and that it was impossible!

Then, one day a little mountain village in a far away place was destroyed by a hurricane, and the people urgently needed help and supplies. The roads were ruined and there was no place to land an airplane or helicopter. The relief workers were desperate as to what to do. They were willing to try anything to save the people. They kept an **open mind** and listened to every idea. Then they heard about Eudora, and finally agreed to let her help.

That's when Eudora the elephant got her parachute, dived from the airplane, floated to earth like a big white cloud, and brought help to the villagers. Because she was an elephant, Eudora could carry lots of supplies, go where there were no roads, move big rocks and trees, and wade through water and mud to help rescue people.

Everybody had agreed that it was impossible to parachute an elephant, but because of the **open-mindedness** of the relief workers, the hurricane victims were saved and Eudora's dream of parachuting came true.

OPEN-MINDEDNESS • OPEN-MINDEDNESS • OPEN-MINDEDNESS • OPEN-MINDEDNESS • OPEN-MINDEDNESS

When did you show **open-mindedness**?

_____

_____

patience

Wait your turn and in no time
You'll reach the front of any line.

P

Is for Patience

One hot summer's day, Katherine wanted an ice cream cone. She went to her favorite ice cream parlor, but there was a long line ahead of her so she would have to wait her turn.

To pass the time, she made friends with the people around her. Soon, they were all telling stories and playing word games. Just when Katherine had reached the front of the line, she noticed a mother with three little kids, who were fussing and crying in the hot summer sun, so Katherine gave them her place.

The mother was very thankful and her kids stopped crying the minute they got ice cream. Because of her **patience** and since she had been so helpful and polite, the ice cream man said Katherine deserved an extra free scoop with a big red cherry on top.

PATIENCE • PATIENCE • PATIENCE • PATIENCE • PATIENCE • PATIENCE • PATIENCE • PATIENCE • PATIENCE

When did you have to use your **patience**?

_____

_____

_____

quality

When family and friends are happy together,
Life can't possibly get any better.

Q

Is for Quality

There's a beautiful tropical island where they had to cut down the trees and bulldoze the jungle to build the Paradise Resort Hotel. It's a five star **quality** hotel because it has air conditioned rooms, a private golf course, tennis courts, a fitness center, and a private beach with an outside shower so you won't track sand into the hotel.

Every room has a TV and a refrigerator full of sodas and goodies. You can even order your meals sent to your room, so you never have to see or hear others.

On the other side of the island is a jungle full of birds and animals. There's a big old tree called the Family Tree because that's where the monkeys hold their yearly family reunion to share their love and respect for each other. The youngsters play games and have a contest. They show all their best **qualities**, like who can leap the farthest, who can howl the loudest, and who has the longest tail. And when they're tired, they take a nap all together in the shade and the cool breezes under the family tree.

But best of all, the family reunion keeps their family together by sharing **quality** time together.

QUALITY • QUALITY • QUALITY • QUALITY • QUALITY • QUALITY • QUALITY • QUALITY • QUALITY • QUALITY • QUALITY

What are your best **qualities**, and what does **quality** time mean to you?

_____

_____

_____

respect

No matter what color, faith, or kin,
We're all the same under the skin.

R
Is for Respect

We are human beings and we're all different from each other. Our skin can be black, brown, yellow, red, pink, or white. Our hair may be blond, black, brown, gray, or red, and we speak many different languages -- but we're just people.

We each have hopes and dreams; we work, play, and love. We each have families, children, and elders. We have homes and community, but we all share the same home, this earth.

Because we have so many similarities, we should like and **respect** each other. Since we are each different and unique, we should appreciate each other's individuality.

Just as we are different in looks, we have different beliefs and religions. But we have many of the same values: care for family, desire for a peaceful home, and hope for a peaceful future.

Really, when you think about it, we're all different but we are all the same under the skin.

RESPECT • RESPECT • RESPECT • RESPECT • RESPECT • RESPECT • RESPECT • RESPECT • RESPECT • RESPECT

Name three people with different skin color you like and **respect**, and tell why.

_____

_____

_____

self-esteem

She likes to watch her long hair twirl
When she dances in a whirl.

S

Is for Self Esteem

Io Pearl had long beautiful hair, but it took a lot of care. Her mother had to brush it for ten minutes every morning before school. Sometimes, the brush would get stuck in her hair, causing her to say "ouch!"

At school, mean kids would pull her hair and make fun of her name. It made her wish that she didn't have long hair and that her name was different. She stopped feeling good about herself and lost her **self esteem**.

Then one day, she was walking home from her dance lesson when her hair got caught and tangled in a bush. It hurt and she began to cry. Suddenly, a friendly wind blew her hair free and sent her spinning down the street. She spun like a top with her hair dancing like golden ribbons in the wind.

People stopped to cheer her, and the wind sang in her ear, "whirl, whirl, pretty girl with a pretty name, Io Pearl!" From then on, she loved her long hair and her name. She felt very happy with herself and her **self esteem** soared!

SELF ESTEEM • SELF ESTEEM • SELF ESTEEM • SELF ESTEEM • SELF ESTEEM • SELF ESTEEM • SELF ESTEEM

What do you like most about yourself?

_____

_____

_____

trust

Have faith in me, and you won't sink;
You are safer than you think.

T

Is for Trust

Sammy wanted to jump off the diving board like the other kids, but was scared. Sammy's dad encouraged him to jump in the water and to **trust** that he'd catch him. It took all of Sammy's courage to walk and finally to crawl the long way to the end of the board. Sammy's dad was patiently waiting. Sammy was so scared that his knees were shaking, his throat was dry, and his eyes were as big as saucers.

Sammy **trusted** his dad, got the courage, and jumped. His dad caught him easily with his big hands and they laughed. This was so much fun that he kept on jumping into his dad's arms. After a while, Sammy began jumping all by himself. His dad stayed close by so that Sammy could see him and feel safe.

Sammy's **trust** in his dad gave him courage to not be afraid and to **trust** himself. He kept jumping until the pool closed. It was the most fun he'd ever had. On the way home, his dad nicknamed him "Froggy."

TRUST • TRUST • TRUST • TRUST • TRUST • TRUST • TRUST • TRUST • TRUST • TRUST • TRUST • TRUST • TRUST

Who do you **trust** more than anyone, and why?

_____

_____

_____

uniqueness

You're not a copy or a clone;
You're very special on your own.

U

Is for Uniqueness

Rudy wasn't like other Rhinos. He was different and **unique** because he wanted to play the piano. But he was told his feet were too big, and that the piano keys were made for little human fingers not big rhinoceros feet.

When conductor Jaime Fondos heard about Rudy, he was so fascinated that he wrote a "Piano Concerto for Rhino." Then the conductor and Rudy decided to have a benefit concert for Rudy's friends and family, the endangered black rhinos.

After sitting on and crushing the piano bench, Rudy sat on the floor and gently put his big front feet onto the keyboard and began to play. Never before had the audience heard such a dramatic piece of music. His big feet made the piano sound like thunder and made the auditorium quake and shake. The audience was so thrilled that at the end of the concerto, they gave Rudy a standing ovation. The audience generously gave money to buy a big park in Africa to save Rudy's friends, the endangered black rhinos.

Rudy's **uniqueness** made him so special that he was able to help his fellow rhinos and to make a new kind of music for everyone's ears.

UNIQUENESS • UNIQUENESS • UNIQUENESS • UNIQUENESS • UNIQUENESS • UNIQUENESS • UNIQUENESS

What makes you different and **unique** from others?

_____

_____

_____

vision

Plan ahead, and the future beams;
Remember, there are no small dreams.

V

Is for Vision

Bart was only a teenager but he had a dream of being the first human to go to Mars. He knew that astronauts had to be good in science and math, so he studied hard and did his homework every night. He remained focused and determined all through high school and college, and graduated with good grades.

To prepare for being an astronaut, he joined the Navy and became a jet pilot. On one flight from his aircraft carrier, he was suddenly caught in a big storm. Lightning struck his plane, destroying his radio, radar and computer. He was lost at night over a big ocean, and low on fuel. By using his math skills, the stars and his watch, he was able to calculate his speed, and the speed, distance, and direction of his aircraft carrier. It took time and patience, but he found his ship and was able to land safely.

When NASA learned of Bart's cool actions in a dangerous situation, they asked him to become an astronaut and train for a future trip to Mars. He had fulfilled his greatest dream because of his **vision** and determination.

VISION • VISION • VISION • VISION • VISION • VISION • VISION • VISION • VISION • VISION • VISION • VISION • VISION

What are your hopes, dreams and **visions** of your future?

_____

_____

_____

willingness

Be ready to help and eager to go;
Whether day or night, rain or snow.

W

Is for Willingness

Sukak and his family were Eskimos who lived in the far north. They lived a long way from the nearest town. His only transportation was his sled and dog team. He always had to stay alert of the weather to make sure his family had enough food and supplies in case they got snowed in.

One day Sukak knew a big snow storm was coming, so he dressed in his warmest clothes and hurried outside to harness his dogs onto the sled to go to the store for supplies. It was already snowing, and the wind was blowing hard; in fact, Sukak couldn't even see his dogs because they had buried themselves deep into the snow to sleep and stay warm.

He whistled for them to come, but there was no sign of his dogs. Finally, a little black nose poked through the snow, and a tail began to wag, throwing the snow in all directions. His big lead dog "Beaver" leaped from his snowy bed and bounded for Sukak's sled. Though he called again and again, Sukak's other dogs stayed sound asleep under their blankets of snow.

Sukak now knew he could trust Beaver's **willingness** to help, and together, off they dashed for supplies before the big storm came. Beaver earned his new name: "Eager Beaver."

WILLINGNESS • WILLINGNESS • WILLINGNESS • WILLINGNESS • WILLINGNESS • WILLINGNESS • WILLINGNESS

When did you show your **willingness** to cooperate and help others?

_____

_____

(e)Xcellence

When you do the best you can,
You're sure to feel like a superman.

X

Is for (e)Xcellence

There was a lot of excitement at the Summer Olympic Games. Three of the best swimmers in the world were competing with each other that day.

The Australian swimmer was the world's record holder for the free-style, the American for the backstroke, and the Japanese for the butterfly and breaststroke. They, along with swimmers from many other countries, were competing in the individual medley race, using a different stroke for each length of the pool.

When each of the record holders swam their best stroke it was really exciting because they would pass all the others. The competition was fun to watch. But though everyone tried his best, the Australian finally won the gold medal for first place. The American won the silver medal for second, and the Japanese won the bronze for third.

All three swimmers showed **excellence** in their best stroke, and not only won medals but the respect of all the other swimmers.

EXCELLENCE • EXCELLENCE • EXCELLENCE • EXCELLENCE • EXCELLENCE • EXCELLENCE • EXCELLENCE

In what endeavor would you like to achieve **excellence**?

_____

_____

_____

Youthful

Playing games and having fun
Helps keep you fit and feeling young.

Y

Is for Youthful

Trevor loves it when Grandpa Mike comes to visit. He always brings a surprise or wears a disguise to make everybody laugh.

Sometimes Grandpa Mike brings his mitt and they go outside to play catch, or shoot baskets on the patio. After dinner, Grandpa Mike shows Trevor some card tricks and Trevor shows Grandpa Mike a computer game. Then Grandpa Mike will romp in the living room with Trevor's little brother and sister. They love for him to give them horseback rides.

At bedtime, Grandpa Mike likes to read all of his grandkids a story and tuck them in.

Some grandpas are happy just to sit and read the paper or watch TV, but not Grandpa Mike. He loves to play and have fun. He says that being with his grandkids keeps him **youthful**!

YOUTHFUL • YOUTHFUL • YOUTHFUL • YOUTHFUL • YOUTHFUL • YOUTHFUL • YOUTHFUL • YOUTHFUL • YOUTHFUL

Name and describe an adult who is fun and acts **youthful**.

_____

_____

_____

Zest

Dolphins love to splash and leap;
They wear a smile as they squeak.

Z

Is for Zest

Ms. Cole's class took a field trip to the aquarium to learn about dolphins. There was a round tank of water where the dolphins were kept, and all they could do was swim in circles all day.

When the students wrote their reports about their field trip to the aquarium, they said they loved seeing the dolphins but felt sorry for them and had empathy for them because the dolphins were not free to frolic in their big ocean home.

The students' next field trip was to study dolphins in the ocean. They took a big boat out of the harbor and out to sea. Very soon they saw a large pod (family) of bottlenose dolphins. There were adult and baby dolphins **zestfully** leaping and diving all around the boat. If you stood at the front of the boat, the dolphins would surf the bow wave and turn on their sides to look right up at you.

The students enjoyed seeing the dolphins at the aquarium and in the ocean, but wished all the dolphins could be free in their natural ocean home where they were so playful and full of **zest**.

ZEST • ZEST • ZEST • ZEST • ZEST • ZEST • ZEST • ZEST • ZEST • ZEST • ZEST • ZEST • ZEST • ZEST • ZEST • ZEST

What makes you feel joyful and full of **zest**?

_____

_____

_____

More Ethics Words!

**Here are more words of ethics and values.
See which ones you know and can spell.**

Allegiance
Apologetic
Assistance

Behavior
Beliefs
Brave

Character
Confidence
Consideration

Dedication
Dignity
Diplomacy

Earnest
Efficiency
Effort

Fairness
Frankness
Friendship

Genuine
Goodness
Gratitude

Helpful
Honorable
Humane

Industrious
Inspirational
Intelligent

Joyful
Judgment
Just

Kindness
Kinship
Knowledgeable

Legality
Listening
Loyalty

Maturity
Moderation
Morality

Neatness
Nice
Noble

Obedient
Obey
Obligation

Pardon
Politeness
Promises

Qualification
Questioning
Quiet

Respectful
Responsibility
Right

Self-control
Sincerity
Strong

Tact
Truthful
Thoughtful

Understanding
United
Unspoiled

Valiant
Vibrant
Vigilance

Warmhearted
Wholesome
Wise

(E)xuberance

Yearning
Yes
Yield

Zealous
Zippy

Can you think of some more?

_____
_____
_____
_____
_____
_____
_____

About the Author

Photo by Saren Brown

James "Bud" Bottoms with his dog, "Tag"

James "Bud" Bottoms is a former teacher, illustrator and sculptor. He has written and illustrated several children's books on environmental issues. On January 28, 1969 in response to the disastrous oil blowout in the Santa Barbara Channel, he helped to spark the "Environmental Revolution."

He has created monumental sculptures and fountains in the U. S., Ireland, Japan, and Mexico. He is best known for his sculpture of three leaping dolphins at the foot of Stearns Wharf in his hometown of Santa Barbara, California. James is the proud father of four sons, stepfather of two daughters, and grandfather of eight grandchildren. His wife, the Reverend Carole Ann Cole, is a Unitarian Universalist minister.

For more information about James "Bud" Bottoms and his work, visit www.dolphinfamily.com.

ALSO AVAILABLE FROM
SUMMERLAND PUBLISHING

Have you ever contemplated how to go about explaining the concept of integrity to a five year old? Don't you wish children would have a better understanding of the core values so often eluding them in today's society, *especially in the face of all of the unethical actions taking place in our capitol these days?* Bud Bottoms, an internationally acclaimed sculptor of ocean life, has written a book called *Kid Ethics* that responds to this void in a child's education. Summerland Publishing has now released *Kid Ethics 2*, a follow-up to the original *Kid Ethics*, both of which can make a major impact on the world.

While *Kid Ethics* is geared towards children ages 5-10, it can be enlightening for the whole family. Mr. Bottoms takes the letters of the alphabet and assigns an ethic to each. Things like honesty, justice and open-mindedness are explained with short stories to which everyone can relate. They are accompanied by the author's pleasant illustrations that can be colored in by the reader. A two-line poem then summarizes the ethic, making it easier to digest. Release Date: 4/23/07. U.S.$12.95/Can. $17.95   ISBN: 978-0-9794863-1-9

"Eliza's Wish" is the third book in the Dickey Denton series. It's the story of Dickey Denton and the mystery he and his friends uncover at Rocky Neck Lighthouse and the Josiah Wheeler mansion. Spurned on by his vivid imagination and his need to discover the truth about the woman who walks the widow's walk, he seeks guidance from his grandfather.

Reluctant at first to give in to Dickey's wishes, Grandpa eventually relents and suggests he seek advice from the spirit of his great-great-grandmother, Eliza Tuffett. Unsure of what to expect, he summons up his courage and decides to risk it.

With the help of his friends, they embark on the adventure and their curiosity takes them back to Rocky Neck Lighthouse and to the haunted Josiah Wheeler mansion on a mysterious journey they'll never forget.

U. S. $14.95 / CAN $19.95   ISBN: 978-0-9794863-8-8